I0491487

PATH TO FINANCIAL SUCCESS

HOW TO ACHIEVE TRUE FINANCIAL FREEDOM

PATH TO FINANCIAL SUCCESS-HOW TO ACHIEVE TRUE FINANCIAL FREEDOM

INDEX

HOW TO ACHIEVE TRUE FINANCIAL FREEDOM

Chapter 1: What Financial Freedom Means

Chapter 2: Realities of Financial Independence

Chapter 3: Begin Your Journey to Financial Freedom

Chapter 4: Tips to Ensure a Successful Financial Independence Plan

Chapter 5: Working Toward Financial Independence

Chapter 6: New trends towards financial management

Chapter 7: Money Matters

Chapter 8: Distinguishing Between Wants and Needs in Life to Achieve Financial Freedom

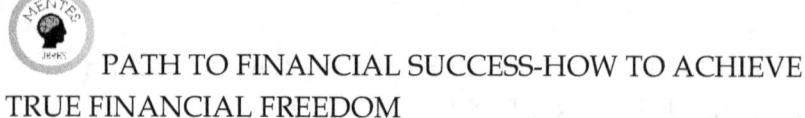

PATH TO FINANCIAL SUCCESS

BOOK 1

PATH TO FINANCIAL SUCCESS

Prelude

This book is designed to meet the needs of people who want to reach greater heights by implementing very simple but powerful concepts that have the potential to change their lives completely.

It is not intended to be a book based on hypothetical research or a philosophical treatise, but it is a book that discovers information that will bring a lasting incentive that will allow us to release internal resources from the force and dynamics of the will.

In fact, it is a compilation of facts presented in simple profane English that contains information that will bring immense joy and success in your life.

It encompasses deep and dynamic truths transmitted in a few powerful words that ignite a renewed sense of awareness of our unlimited latent inner resources waiting to burst into the open. It encompasses practical expressions that have the potential to bring success, health, wealth and lasting happiness.

LET'S START....

One of the most difficult points to reconcile in life is the paradox that suffering exists in this world. Suffering is eminent.

Of course, what is equally important is to realize that the acquisition and possession of wealth is not a ruler who measures one's happiness. If joy were really to be found in materials, then all those who experience their "emotion" in contact with the object would observe the same measure of joy.

In life, men are continually motivated by two unavoidable impulses of repulsion: from pain and craving to the pursuit of joy and absolute realization. In the pursuit of happiness, he is forced to run after the pleasant and pleasant, while when confronted with the opposite, he avoids undesirable objects and unpleasant environments.

The fact is this: throughout history, all those who have achieved success consciously or unconsciously have used five principles, which are common to absolute progress in all aspects of life.

The 5 principles for unlocking wealth

These principles are the key to unlocking the incredible reservoir of wealth, abundance and success. They are all focused on our true innate qualities, which are in fact universal and spiritually grounded. These principles are:

- The Truth
- Justice
- Peace
- Love
- Nonviolence

The practice of these virtues will enable

anyone to progress in life without any doubt.

The reason is simple.

These universal principles are all attractive and, of course, constitute the cornerstones of the code of ethics. You cannot make a mistake practicing the importance of moral values, codes of conduct, and obeying the Law of Nature in your quest for Wealth.

In the following pages, you will discover the goal of achieving financial freedom while, at the same time, acquiring the perfect art of happiness through the understanding that the measure of joy is not `directly' proportional to just monetary wealth.

This concise, accurate, direct-to-the-point manuscript explores avenues that will definitely change your life for the better.

Unlike many other books on the same subject, this manuscript delves into thematic areas relevant to aspects of your personal life and growth that I can guarantee will bring that smile back to your face. It is a clear, focused and above all legible book that you will like.

Can it never happen?

While pessimism warns us of the dangers
lurking before our very eyes, optimism can
lead to false security. Pessimism should only
be considered initial and not a final
predicament in any situation - this is the first
step towards success.

Again and again, we have been subject to
instances that are disturbing, and deep
within ourselves we realize the dangers and
potential risks that surround us, and the
voice categorically rejects this threatening
situation that confronts us, as such, because
we do not recognize this voice, our mental
clinging to the outside world moves us away
from the inner voice of TRUTH, which takes

us totally off the tracks so to speak.

The second step towards success and wealth is to convince oneself of the importance of self-control, self-consciousness and self-discipline.

We must listen to the inner voice and realize the existence of the innate force or Dynamic Will - the powerful power it expresses through the mind, body and intellect! Therefore, the second step qualifies you to develop faith not only in what you can do and accomplish, but above all in the development of faith itself (its innate, inherent and latent qualities).

The third step requires that through constant vigilance, employing the power of intelligence, self-analysis and introspection, and through understanding and careful use of these concepts, you can learn to live beyond the demands of the mind in whatever environment you are in - this will qualify you to implement and embrace the path to wealth.

There is no such thing as a free lunch. If you hate to do any work/effort but love to succeed, you will have to reconsider your views.

So to achieve the latter, you have to do the first thing and the sensible idea is to find out what really gives you pleasure and then find out if it is possible to make money out of it.

"If you don't start, you won't succeed."

Pursuing wealth

The statement "haste makes waste true even today, and most of the time, some of us tend to feel frustrated when we cannot live up to our ideals and the standards we set for ourselves all the time.

At other times, we may feel that if we had accepted the challenge presented to us, perhaps things would have changed for the better, but there is also the possibility that in our over-anxiousness to reach the goal we will try too hard and burn ourselves to the ground.

Has this happened to you?

The question that remains to be asked is: how do we begin, how do we achieve success in life?

Well, my friend, rest assured that this book has been written to answer this question satisfactorily, eliminating any confusion or anomaly.

There are many strategies that one can employ and various means by which one can plow to reach the goal. A common trait in all of them is self-belief, self-righteousness or honesty and ethical living (in words, deeds, thoughts and actions) that pertain to your

lifestyle - this is the fourth step.

In any business, the emphasis on moral and ethical standards is the highest, and this should not be ignored or overlooked.

The only way to achieve equanimity, balance or equilibrium, even after becoming the richest individual, is to have a sense of realizing the true essence of life.

Nothing in life is constant. Life is always changing and things that seem to exist today may cease to exist tomorrow and this is a fact that you - and everyone else - must learn to accept.

Step five, when you discover something deep

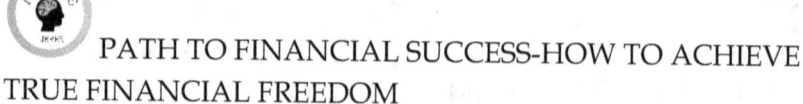
and beautiful, the natural tendency is to share it with others.

In the following chapters what you will discover are the true ways to achieve complete success, and this is a book that will allow you to unleash your innate qualities in the foreground, allowing you to reap the benefits and rewards that thousands of people around the world are enjoying right now because they have become rich.

Following the guide within the following pages, and I sincerely believe that each person has the potential to succeed in life.

"Wealth is more than just money.

The Ladder to Success

It is man's privilege to attain total greatness, and in reality success should be everyone's habit. Man is essentially perfect, and therefore infinite are the possibilities which lie dormant in him.

To get the best out of our inner self, an organized and perfectly disciplined life for the discovery of the potentials that lie in wait for us, is a well spent life.

The vital point is not how many talents each of us has, but the importance must focus on how many of our existing talents, attributes and capabilities we are prepared to develop, exploit, explore and implement in our daily lives.

The question you must ask yourself is whether you are making practical use of at least one great talent inherent in you. The only supreme fundamental principle is to understand that all our success depends entirely on ourselves.

The best way to be happy is to do the things you naturally love and enjoy doing - something you are absolutely passionate about! In the same way, the best way to succeed and get rich is to make sure that you achieve the things you have sincerely wanted to look for in life. This will require you to implement your efforts in activities that allow you to measure success.

For example, the simple way to explain this is to take into consideration the following example: if you like art, painting and drawing, then the way to proceed is to seek guidance on ways to participate in contests, and ways to present your artwork through galleries (approaching galleries directly and leaving your work for sale or in exchange) or art publishers or even exhibit your talent by participating in seasonal fairs where you will find a lot of all kinds of retailers.

You may want to add several different types of themes to your art portfolio in order to maximize your ability to reach a wide audience with interests in different themes.

Contact groups, forums and even

newsgroups on the Internet and explore other avenues (such as photographers, photo galleries and frames, art tips and government organizations that provide help, including loans, etc.) that will allow you to intensify your research - the idea is to pursue the goal relentlessly and with a positive attitude.

When it comes to your topic, post questions, surveys, polls and determine what people are looking for, and then simply find the need and fill it out.

Every little detail will help, but it's the force needed to get the momentum going and that's the key point. Another useful point is not simply to try, try and keep trying, but to develop an attitude in which you do what you have decided to do, implement and apply the strategies shown in this book.

Finally, don't limit yourself to that: keep the faith and don't give in to any defeat. Once you've decided to put the "plan" into action, make sure it stays lit and bright...rejections and disappointments should in no way reduce your hope, your progress, and your desire for success. People who have succeeded despite all the difficulties, pain and struggle have inspired countless millions of people around the world - it's time for you to set an example for others to follow in your footsteps as well.

You must remember that the methods employed by different individuals in obtaining wealth may be different, but the goal is common to all, and the steps mentioned above are indeed your tools for overall success.

It takes a very strong willpower to develop internally, and the need for two very important attributes, namely courage and trust, are essential ingredients. Thus, poverty and prosperity do not necessarily depend on knowledge as a whole (e.g., business acumen, marketing strategies, etc.), but certainly depend on the three Cs and are character, creativity and innate abilities.

Courage and confidence alone can produce a unique transformation, while the opposite will only bring much pain and despair in times of distress and crisis. However, despite life's problems, we must resist obstacles and obstacles and, as such, constantly remind ourselves of the inherent or innate supreme power that we all possess and that we can all successfully develop through spiritual discernment. Therefore, ignoring our abilities and potential to develop the personal power we need to go through ego-breaking experiences requires immense strength and discipline, and I explain to you in this book how you could accomplish all of this here and now.

Without these qualities you are destined to fail, and that is why a lot of people feel discouraged because they entered into competition or simply surrendered under pressure, for lack of self-motivation and lack of dynamic willpower.

When our fantasies and expectations are not met, there is a tendency for us to return to our old ways - the emptiness we experience can be very annoying and we cannot ignore it forever. Often what happens exactly is that whatever good we do in life does not mean that we will continue. This is not because an impossible discipline is required, but because we lack courage and confidence, we are overwhelmed with a negative attitude - this is what stops everything in its path!

The initial burst of enthusiasm begins to fade, and what seemed so wonderful become a danger, a dilemma, and a problem. The mind takes over and the questions overcome the doubts that arise after the idea or whole concept is worthwhile - a conflict occurs, the mind says one thing and the intellect and our intuition impels us to follow the path to `success'.

Even before we begin the journey the end is imminent, because we are undecided about the true path to follow. Success lies in what you make of it, not in what you 'think' it should be (don't fantasize about success).

So how do we get started?

Formula for success

What you think and how you act is the decisive factor that will help you discover the goal of success. These two attributes are important along with a set of consistent principles, which you must follow. Thoughts based on reason are a powerful catalyst for initiating any reaction, and once you get going, you will soon realize that courage is the simple virtue necessary for a human being to cross the rocky path.

The obstacles are natural, and are a means to the source of wealth acquisition, as I am sure you will agree. Persistence, patience and perseverance will have to be practiced religiously to reach the goal and overcome the obstacles. Of course, having said that, I would now like to point out the P's that you should disapprove of.

Don't put it off, don't pretend you know everything and finally don't prolong your 'enterprise(s)'. Be prepared to fight the obstacles that may confront you, but pursue your goal and allow your potential willpower to predominate.

In any life situation, it is unequivocally important to keep your head level, despite all the "ups and downs" you are likely to face. Remember that life is dualistic by nature - the obverse and reverse of the same coin to put it simply. I am obliged to add that although we know that the past is the cause and the present is the effect, it is evident that with time the present itself becomes the cause with

33

reference to the future.

There is a very deep meaning entangled in this syntax, and if it can be related to success, then it can be said that if we live intelligently in scientific self-discipline, we can become the architects of our own future.

The Basic Steps

The following guidelines will help pave the way to ultimate success.

The steps are very simple to implement in your daily life.

1. Do what you love and what you are good at.

2. Be prepared to learn and be positive (motivation and enthusiasm).

3. Be an innovative individual.

4. Be prepared to invest not only money, but also time, effort and resources.

I've mentioned money - this doesn't mean you have to invest a large sum to become a millionaire or rich.

5. You must be disciplined in setting goals and objectives. Remember that persistence is the key to success.

6. You must be prepared to manage your time effectively.

7. As you evolve, learn to return what you love to society. I call this philanthropy.

You must have a solid vision - one in which you see yourself having achieved success. Great people of the past and present see to it that they achieve this coveted position by employing these basic steps.

However, note that in step 2 I deliberately used the word `learn', and that too for a very good reason. Life is the greatest teacher, so you must be willing to accept challenges all the time (using the power of discrimination) and as a result you must learn through its eternal principles the magnificent doctrine that it has revealed over time. This means that you must act at the right time.

Action is incredibly important and highlights success: both are synonymous with honesty.

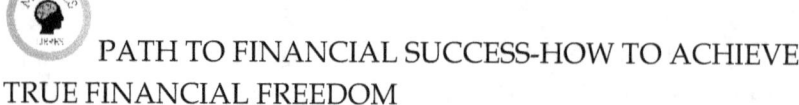

Success requires action, but the essential ingredient is seriousness. Being too serious can ruin your business, so the point is to have fun.

Any discipline will require organization and order. As I mentioned in the introduction, you must be prepared to listen to your inner voice as much as you can. This means that instead of relying too much on your family, friends, etc. (it's not that this is bad) start having faith in your own abilities.

On your own and strive to learn and succeed. Often, failures can be the result of cases where we have stopped exercising our own views or have become too dependent on those of others.

Success is not a secret you have to seek or dig up to reach your destination; it is rather the understanding or recognition factor you develop regarding what you really want in life. Intuition, courage, skills, knowledge, challenges and opportunities are some of the concepts that determine the traits of people who enjoy wealth. Any task done with the right spirit will give you victory. Mental attitude is what will give you success, but negative attitude, laziness and involuntary work will result in failure.

Don't wait too long in a short time, but your approach should be positive and execute your task with absolute perfection, paying special attention to your long-term goal(s). This means that you approach your duty with concentrated energy and execute your plans with uprightness. This should be your philosophy of life.

To start a new venture, it is vitally important that you realize the following, which I have to say is crucial. You have to appreciate the fact that to start a business you need to become familiar with the term cash flow. Investment in the form of capital is a requirement, but the most important thing is the concept of business viability.

Steps towards personal wealth

Decision-making is perhaps the most difficult step in your quest to begin the journey to wealth. The problem is that until you go deeper into yourself to unlock your innate qualities, the chances are that you will be indecisive and hesitant. This is not bad as such, but most of the time this "feeling" may not allow you to maximize your full potential.

There is no secret to releasing your full potential - the "secret" lies in your willingness to listen to your inner voice. The initiative to seize a good opportunity presented to you is to undertake the task in a methodical way.

Sit quietly, calm your senses and thoughts, and meditate deeply on the subject in question. Don't jump into anything at once just because the idea seems favorable. Most things seem very "good" in the initial phase, but thinking, planning, and having time is a prerequisite. It's often something inside you that will tell you what to do. The secret is not necessarily from the outside, but can be acquired from the inside.

Striving to do your best at all times is the little secret that will help you accumulate wealth. Imagination (that is, constructive imagination), which is the power to visualize, is an important factor in creative thinking - but as you can see, it will not be possible to do this without a strong will, and above all this faculty of visualization has to mature into a firm belief and conviction.

1. You must have the desire to reach your goal of fame - this is rule number one.

2. Be prepared to manage money efficiently with respect to budget, expenses and responsibility and/or accountability.

3. Do not spend more than you are required to and spend less than you earn.

4. Personal problems, including not only drug addiction, etc., can be ruinous. This is something to deal with from the beginning.

5. Discover ways to invest and, above all, start saving money. You'll have to play smart and have your priorities absolutely right.

In any company, you are likely to face a great antagonism, far from an idealistic situation. Above and beyond expectations, optimism and a tendency to "want" things to work as planned, it can and often can lead to failure.

Therefore, as mentioned above, planning is very important to your success. Of course, the other factors that need to be taken into account are also overwork and burnout. In the hope of making your millions, the likelihood is that you will become a frustrated shipwreck and become a discouragement - this will not be helpful in your progress or pursuit of wealth.

Reaching Your Goal

When you persist in refusing to accept failure, know that the object you have set out to achieve will materialize through dynamic willpower.

Thoughts can be incredibly powerful tools, and if you are willing to implement this divine gift then you are sure to reach your goal. If you cling to a certain thought with dynamic willpower, it assumes a tangible outer form.

Now is the time to cauterize the inherent negative characteristics in the form of habits, lack of willpower, lack of trust, hesitation,

45

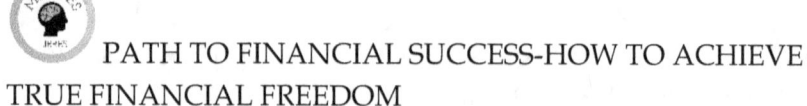
and wrong attitude toward life in general. You have within you the power to achieve everything you want, that power resides in the will. The main cause of failure in life is lack of concentration - do not accumulate with ideas, concepts, and strategies all at once in the hope of success. Start slowly and be consistent in your goal-setting scheme.

Focus your attention on one thing at a time, and don't allow your MIND to enter a state of "overload. There is a scientific way to use concentration, and the magic word is to remain calm, while performing all your tasks with the right speed.

DO NOT rush and create chaos, but rather approach methodically and meticulously and focus your whole mind on what you undertake, and the important thing is to keep your mind flexible.

Once you know that you are really on the right track and on the road to achieving your goal, be careful about time management. It is often very easy to get so involved in a project that you can get carried away with perfecting whatever you are doing.

You must priorities your work and above all respect and honour the value of time - don't waste your time and your life!

The keys to success

As I have already mentioned, the environment plays a very important role, as it is quite inevitable, especially our indoor environment.

A calm and relaxed individual is much more likely to emerge victorious in a difficult situation than his counterpart - a person whose nerves are frustrated and erratic. The former has his senses fully identified with the environment in which he is situated.

However, the restless individual does not understand the environment and consequently gets into trouble. The key words are focus, concentration and care in everything you do in life.

1. Develop a defined and well-defined goal/objective.

2. Develop an intelligent and workable plan/program.

3. Take care of your health. Without health there is no real wealth.

4. You must conserve your energy.

5. Be honest in your life (in words, deeds, thoughts and actions).

6. Stick to virtues and adopt good principles.

7. Reflect on ideal personalities and seek the strength of your philosophy.

8. Seek divine guidance and be sincere.

9. Strive to help and serve others with gratitude.

10. Always think positive and believe in God's power.

Transformative thinking is indeed the way to success. Establish a plan to reach your goal and deliberately ruminate on the meaning of this plan and make it a reality.

Since time immemorial, great people from all walks of life have emerged as true victors, and the reason behind this is to train the mind for happiness. Ethical discipline is essential, particularly self-discipline.

Each individual is unique. What is good for person A may not be suitable for person B. However, it must be emphasized that everyone can enjoy stillness, solitude and silence, and to be honest each individual, regardless of age, caste, creed, color, sex, has experienced at some stage or another peace.

After discovering through the trial and error method, you can determine the precise way to compose your mind-body complex and thus reach great heights.

Meditation may not be effective for everyone, but that does not mean that you do not improvise such methods as and when necessary.

Be systematic, and your only goal should be to employ methods that bring you success and happiness.

Our mental faculties determine our actions, and it is quite obvious that the mind must be tamed and subdued. Constant vigilance is necessary, and continuous training of the mind will pave the way to ultimate success.

Do not fall prey to the dictates of your mind!

Optimistic, heroic and noble ideals have a

powerful and edifying effect upon the body. Enthusiasm with deliberate and well-orchestrated self-application in a cheerful state of mind and absolute optimism is the secret path to wealth for all great men.

The Power of Thoughts

The previous chapter highlighted the importance of cultivating the right attitude and developing faith in what one seeks to achieve in life.

Nothing in life is impossible unless you believe it. Thoughts are remarkable 'packages' of energy and if you cling tenaciously to a certain thought with dynamic willpower, there is no reason why this thought cannot manifest according to the plane you have created.

I mentioned earlier briefly in explaining how a person interested in art can increase their abilities to excel in life. Now I will use the same example to illustrate the power of thought. An artist develops an idea to create a painting or a drawing of a beautiful landscape.

The thought process initiates a series of ideas and the artist then uses them to produce the skeleton work, allowing him to complete the final work of art according to the mental plane initially created. A mere thought process allows the artist to create the masterpiece!

This creation is itself a scientific principle based on the Universal Law of Creation. It is the source from which everything manifests. It is in all of us, and it can certainly be harnessed if you are willing to try. The secret is not really a secret, but it is a treasure hidden within each and every one of us and we have the right to use it in the most effective way.

Isn't it true that when you see someone so happy and euphoric, your mind becomes entangled with joy and you discover that there is a smile on your face?

Thoughts are so closely woven into the mind. If the thoughts are calm, the mind is calm. In any aspect of life, whether it's starting a business, getting your first job or getting married, the relationship between mind and thought is most important.

Systematically, therefore, we must train and discipline the mind for right thinking and diligent activity, and thus have a correct understanding of what you really want in life, and how this will add to the effective dynamism in your quest and what you ultimately seek - your path to success and wealth will become graceful, meaningful and attainable!

People with certain qualities are attracted almost magnetically, and such qualities are called positive qualities. These qualities are present in all of us, but are not clearly invoked or understood. We know what love, kindness, courage and joy mean, they are noble virtues, and we also recognize them as qualities we admire in others.

Even though we know this, when we act, we act by compromising ideals. The reason behind this is that we are never faithful to ourselves - we are constantly acting and

putting on a show to please everyone around us, let alone ourselves! It's painful, demoralizing and quite agonizing not to be your true self.

You can incredulously exclaim, and sit down, what does this have to do with wealth and prosperity? I acknowledge your concern, but I humbly ask you to take a moment or two, and in the silence of the night reflect deeply upon this point. I would like you to put into practice what I mentioned earlier by being yourself.

Notice the changes that occur with the passage of time, and what you will truly discover is that when one can express the fragrance of your innate positive qualities or characteristics (of who you really are), then not only people but all things that you have always wanted or desired will come to you.

"Like thought, so is mind."

In order to fulfill your goals and dreams, it is necessary to practice what the book describes.

The habitual inclination of our thought patterns is ultimately the decisive factor that determines our abilities, talents and personal characteristics. Based on this critical and vital knowledge, one assumes that those fortunate few were born with the special talent that you lack and fervently desire to have.

This is largely true, but it must be said that no one is born a millionaire, period! The valuable information lies in the art of cultivating the pattern that brings success. We are what we think we are.

It is true when the Masters say, "Your thoughts create the environment.

- Thoughts develop personality
- Thoughts promote health
- Thoughts influence the body
- Thoughts can change and shape the future (destiny)
- Thoughts bring creation
- Thoughts influence people's physiology and psychology
- Thoughts can bring success
- Thoughts can even heal the body

Watch your thoughts constantly. Their

experiences and the environment have their "seat" in the thoughts.

Your suggestion and self-suggestion through meditation and visualization techniques should be stronger than the thoughts, and when your actions elevate you, know that you have understood the art of controlling your thought processes.

You can accomplish anything through the power of thought. Visualization uses your imagination to allow you to 'imagine' your success or achieve your serious goal.

Your thoughts or mental vibrations are incredibly powerful, because the mind has a tangible connection to your thoughts and actions. Its thoughts are subtle energies and have a strong connection to our consciousness.

Therefore, constant feeding of positive thoughts through visualization, yoga and meditation will bring harmony, happiness, health and wealth!

Factors that cause inertia

First and foremost is introspection, and this literally means that you take stock of your traits and habits.

Often, the lack of self-analysis is the cause of our short fall, and it is the lack of a definite, indivisible effort and attention that stands in your way toward progress and the achievement of your desired goal.

Therefore, introspection means re-evaluating our mental "block" and diagnosing deficiencies by eliminating negative tendencies in the form of habits, indecision, fear, lack of trust, etc., which we often call

failures.

It is time to revitalize yourself so that by uprooting all these negativities from your life, true happiness with the zeal to progress becomes prominent and firmly rooted.

The greatest enemy that prevents us from advancing in life apart from apathy, lack of trust and inferiority complex is FEAR. Fear will literally keep us from moving forward - in fact, we won't even meet our goal of success. The best way to combat fear is to practice deep breathing exercises, and every night mentally affirms that you are under the protection of the supreme personality of divinity, and energize your thoughts with positive feelings.

Consciously uproot the seeds of fear from within through a forced concentration on courage, and change your consciousness to a level that allows you to fully appreciate that you are beyond any kind or class of pain. Fear comes from the heart, so fill your heart with LOVE, and when you feel agitated relax, calm down and breathe rhythmically, relaxing with each exhalation.

Of course there is another problem, which I believe is the main cause of frustration and which subsequently diminishes our ability to excel in life. It is what I call "desirous of results without the will to make the effort. I personally have failed because of such a negative outlook, and I am the first to admit it openly.

Now, this is where it becomes clear what I

have said before. Failure, pain, disease and insufficiencies are natural eventualities when the Law of Nature is broken.

Transgression and violation of the eternal law of nature brings misery. As human beings we have the capacity to shape, correct and change our lives, goals and destiny.

The greatest impediment you will encounter in your life is your immediate environment. If there is something that you will have to change - you may have noticed that I started this book sounding a little cynical and a little overly cautious, much less a little negative - the main reason for this will now become evident.

The environment I have just mentioned can

be defined in two, namely the interior and the exterior. It is these two fields of the environment that you will have to be aware of.

All your experiences come from your mental things - or from the inner environment (thoughts). What you perceive through all your senses from the outside will also shape your future.

Therefore, the important point here is to watch your thoughts. My suggestion is to be careful with your inner environment rather than your outer environment. For example, you may have come across a great home business opportunity that is potentially excellent and fair to you in every respect.

You are happy and willing to try it... but in retrospect, something about this business prevents you from moving forward with it. There may be several reasons for this, but I am very curious to know the main reason. Rest assured that it can't be money (because it's within your budget), nor can it be a hype (because it has apparently worked for thousands of people with testimonials to confirm).

So what am I wondering? Think about this point, and you will no doubt come to a favorable conclusion....and surprisingly it is, things of the mind - the perpetrator.

To succeed in life you will have to start by correcting your thought patterns, because it is the companionship of your thoughts and the affinity you have with them that will determine your destiny.

"Thoughts are expressed through the physical body."

The Risk Factor

Without straying from the subject, I would like to remind you of what I mentioned in the early stages of the book on the dualistic nature of life.

Why is it that some people are so fortunate and others fall behind in the struggle for success?

This is not true, as we all know, however, what makes one person richer than the other depends largely on the choice or decision made, along with the risk or risks recognized through a greater understanding of the power of discrimination and the ability to weigh and balance the scales of one's intuitive faculty.

Now the risk you take has to be one based on the understanding that the company you have chosen to pursue has been thoroughly investigated. You only embark on taking a driving test, for example, once you feel you are competent enough to pass it and not otherwise.

Therefore, the risk you assume in this regard must be what I call an informed risk. In other words, it is one in which you have confidence in what you are getting into, and this is also based on the source of information you have looked for well.

The fact that you are now reading this report

is to understand how to achieve financial success - therefore, this report is somehow your research tool that will allow you to implement the techniques and tips described to achieve the goal. Therefore, the measures taken come directly from a source that can be considered authentic, valuable and genuine.

Once you feel confident that you are going to take the driving test with the guidance of the driving instructor, you decide to take the driving test - this is the perfect way to ensure success. I want to correct an issue that has already been raised above and that has to do with learning.

You must be willing to learn constantly, because to gain any skill, knowledge and power, you must be prepared to **LEARN.**

Commitment is the life force you have to get used to from the beginning. Remember that there are certain situations in which you may not have direct control to bring about any foreseeable change, which can result in a lot of headache.

However, this does not have to be so because what really matters is the mechanism or way in which the situation is controlled and ultimately the way in which one reacts to it.

The problem with us is that we tend to live in the past and in the future at the same time. When our mental faculty is overloaded, we become discouraged.

The burden is too heavy for the mind, so we must restrict it. When we have too much to do at any given time, we must immediately stop our activities. The clock moves at a regular pace, it cannot be twenty-four hours away in sixty seconds, nor can it be done in one hour what can be done most effectively in twenty-four hours. He lives for the now, and the `future' will take care of himself.

Don't be greedy and, above all, don't get burned for 'wanting' to become a millionaire!

Things have changed, more and more people are turning to a simple lifestyle back to the basics - without so many luxuries and less worries.

The dualistic concept of nature prevails

everywhere - you can't prosper if you write checks without having credible funds or credit (deposit) in your bank account, sooner or later you'll run out of money.

Without peace of mind, the likely hood of running out of steam, happiness, calm and strength, you will become a mentally, emotionally, spiritually and physically exhausted 'broken'. What a pity that it will all have been to reach a point of total desolation!

It is then that you must dwell in inner power and mentally affirm your purpose in life; you may want to go through some pleasurable experience so that you completely forget your worries. The point is not to take anything too seriously, to enjoy what you have and to be happy with what is rightfully yours.

What to avoid

It is natural that when the unexpected happens, we are much more likely to react negatively. However, this doesn't have to be so, the book reveals ways to achieve your goal in a harmonious and diligent manner.

The following are some helpful tips:

1. When things go wrong, don't overreact. Think positively and calmly.

2. Don't judge too much, or criticize too much.

3. Try not to ignore a bad situation, be careful with the comfort zone.

4. Wisdom and strength alone can help you overcome many of life's imminent problems.

5. Facing problems head-on.

6. Avoid greed and vanity of any kind.

There is a business ethic and a businessman should practice this ethic. Those who are strictly honest and truthful will prosper in business. Let us once again consider art as an example to highlight what has been discussed so far. As we all know, we have innate powers - within each of us lies the storehouse of latent energy that explodes to be `awakened'.

Suppose you have the creative power, and being an artist, for example, you can virtually paint and draw any theme or theme.

It's fair; it's obvious that you have considerable talent, since not all artists have this ability.

Since you are aware of this, you can assume that because your artwork is good, it has good potential to be sold. That's true, but let's considers all the factors that need to be taken into account step by step.

1. You may be a very good artist, but if your work is not noticed and appreciated, it has no real benefit. Therefore, it is important that your work is noticed (through the maximum exposure) and the way to do it is to establish your name.

This requires you to contact the right sources and approach artists who have gone through the "same" learning curve to reach the path of prosperity. The competition that may exist in the chosen field must be taken into account. You must prepare a good foundation - this can be done by using the information within the pages of this book.

2. Your work of art may be exceptionally beautiful, but without understanding the dynamics of the market your work may not flourish.

3. From your personal perspective, your work may seem to have great potential. However, it is important to appreciate the opinions of the general public, that is, your potential buyers.

Don't get involved in the routine that most people do, "listening to what we want to hear" is a kind of precondition that can bring untold misery.

4. You should look in other areas to develop your potential. Expand the category/theme of the topic, the use of different types of media (e.g. acrylics, oils, mixed media, etc.), decide how to promote your work, you may even want to sell originals or reproduce prints.... The possibilities are endless, the question is how determined you are in your quest for success.

The psychology of success depends on many factors, but what I think is most vital is self-confidence. Most people never get to the first stage of success because they lack this essential characteristic.

Such conditioning often comes from their personal experiences, but the causal factor is the environment, which has already been discussed. While it is good to be cautious about anything you do in life, it is equally essential that you do not become entangled in the technicalities of the "process," but concentrate on the benefits and final reward it produces.

Dedicate your goal to success by implementing the five cardinal words that begin with the letter D to your success, namely, Devotion, Discrimination, Discipline, Determination and Duty.

There is nothing wrong with asking questions about the proposals you are presented with or even about the business opportunities you intend to pursue. As long as these questions provide all the answers and you decide to move forward considering all the factors, then everything is fine and good.

However, when your questions defeat the very purpose of your research, then it becomes a "vicious circle.

Why, what, where, when, who are the words we often use to find out information about everything in life - including business - giving rise to questions.

The question with the word why it is necessary will help us draw a perfect conclusion and help us overcome doubts. The problem with this is that if you are not clear about your goal(s), then the very question by which you want to go ahead with the venture is meaningless.

What you need to keep in mind are the likely long-term goals, the benefits, and how your first step toward wealth and success will allow you to enjoy greater heights.

The inevitable mistakes

As human beings we are very restless - often
overwhelmed by joy, success or gratification.
It is very important to remain calm during
such events, because emotion can lead to
problems, of which one is spending too
much.

That said, it is also very important to realize
that success can simply 'hit' you, in the sense
that you can become complacent and `decide'
not to do much, because `you have it all'.

This is a terrible phase that you may possibly
enter, and that you should be aware of at all
times. However, the only thing you should

be aware of is the ego complex - don't let your ego become an impediment in your effort to attain wealth.

The best medicine to avoid the ego is to conserve energy. The energy that has been generated and conserved, unless directed to the proper channels, will be catastrophic.

We must control our impulses, and this is where the art of practicing life balance becomes an essential tool for your success. Talking without doing anything is a unique factor that can destroy your desire to succeed.

Remember, that the people around you and the company you have will determine your future success - you may lose precious time, but those around you will make it even worse, contributing to the total loss of your own time.

Therefore, as the saying goes, "like attracts like" should be the maxim, and above all use common sense all the time, and only do what produces positive results.

Being systematic will also help to avoid confusion and inconvenience, which can have an adverse effect on your business and your goals. Do not accept jobs that may delay you.

Try to evaluate the situation, giving a lot of importance to priorities - don't leave things for another time, don't waste time and, above all, don't waste your precious energy. If you act carefully, time will be managed in the most efficient way.

If words, deeds, thoughts and actions are good, then life will be good, and every moment will bring success, and the "time" taken to reach the coveted goal will be....well, your guess is as good as mine.

"The mind is the cause of slavery and freedom."

The Law of Success

By simply understanding the common principles, some of which have already been discussed above, one can achieve success.

A conscious effort must be made to provide good experiences for the mind. Nature has provided man with everything in great abundance - sadly though human beings have not realized this fact.

You must decide to succeed. How can he do this effectively?

How can the will be developed? Success

comes with planning, determination and faith without a doubt. To determine this fact I suggest you try the following: Choose some goal that you think you cannot achieve, and then try with all your energy and strength to do that one thing.

This could be anything from drawing a portrait to mastering the use of the computer. When you've achieved success, go to something bigger and keep trying to exercise your willpower. Despite any setback, do not shake yourself, but draw strength from your surroundings and, above all, learn from like-minded people who have courageously pursued success without ever losing hope.

Remember people like Abraham Lincoln, Henry Ford, Mother Teresa, and many more who have reached the coveted position because of their innate power of faith and dynamic will. Remember, you too can achieve the same success.

This law can be applied by anyone and it works. It is true that our thoughts and actions shape our future and destiny. You must be willing to channel your talent and your innate abilities in the right direction, so that you can rise to new heights.

To recapitulate what has been said so far, let me remind you what it takes to succeed.

- Planning is crucial and perhaps the most important step to your success.

- Prepare to change your views, habits and thought patterns.

- They only pursue tasks that are important. You must divide your needs from your desires - there is a very fine line, so exercise discrimination.

- Watch your personal financial situation. Make a good budget and reduce expenses.

- Surround yourself with people with a positive personality and those who are successful. Read books about people who have succeeded in life.

- Don't pretend to be who you are not. Be yourself and don't brag.

- Expand your horizons and be enthusiastic and ambitious.

- It's good to increase your income, but it's even better to invest in assets that will make you rich.

- Prepare to work hard and make sacrifices.

The right actions enrich, strengthen and motivate us, fully vitalizing our internal resources.

Cultivating such values and adhering to the right values of life will help us grow and achieve success.

Such a consistent diet and exposure can shape our character and help redeem our inferior tendencies.

Time to learn who you are

I would disapprove of anyone who came up
with a comment, saying that success is just a
desire.

We are not born failures - let me make this
point clear. We have all succeeded in our
lives at one time or another and this is an
undeniable **TRUTH.**

The following points will surely enable you
to understand who you really are, and that is
a guarantee. Once you figure out your own
attributes, it will be much easier to embrace
ideals that will allow you to jump to higher
heights.

1. Are you generally enthusiastic and positive or quite the opposite?

2. Do you like to work hard and would you try a little harder if you did what you like best?

3. Are you being all you can be? You may want to analyze your strengths and weaknesses.

4. Are you satisfied with your current situation and/or circumstances?

By answering these three very important questions, you can determine your future. Remember the importance of discipline and organization mentioned above.

The next point I want to make is simplicity. Do not create unnecessary difficulties in the path of your work and in the goal of success.

By simplicity I mean, don't complicate the situation, and don't let success go to your head - the pompous attitude is another problem that can bring you down. Be humble, firm, and fair in your efforts to succeed.

A quiet individual can accomplish virtually anything simply through the power of concentration - this is a science-based truth.

Research has clearly shown that techniques

such as yoga, visualization and relaxation can bring greater awareness, allowing the individual to reach his or her full potential.

By the power of concentration and focus, a person can achieve what he or she has desired.

The need for change

We are all very aware that nothing remains permanent in life, despite understanding that life itself is a continuum, what we have not realized is that our own attitudes, conditioning and propensities prevent us from incorporating change.

One of the most difficult things to change is our nature (indelible thoughts), particularly those that have left a mark on our psyche.

We may be able to change many things around us, but the need to change our thoughts, attitudes and habits, which almost certainly have become part of our own identity, becomes an arduous and difficult task.

As with all things in life, time can heal anything and everything - let time help you grow in life and without wasting time to reach your individual goals.

How do we change our mental attitude? The answer is very simple: once again, there is no secret as such, nor is it an arduous task to carry out. The primary answer lies in the word change itself. Initiating gradual changes in your lifestyle will help you reach your goal much faster. I say that the answer is easy with regard to how we can achieve positive change, because we consider, for example, habits.

Habits take time to take root, as we all know. Just as you `learn' your habits over time, you simply begin to unlearn them. Habits are very difficult to eradicate at once, and therefore, you leave time to take care of your habits. What does this have to do with being happy and rich?

Well, my friends, I would like to return the same question to you. Ask yourself why you haven't been able to make progress.

Put into practice what you have gathered so far. Sit in a quiet corner and open your heart, and solve this problem - the answer to all your problems, good or bad, are within you. The accuracy of the problem will no doubt vary, but the reason(s) for it are self-explanatory.

Why it is that person Y is able to quit smoking and yet person Z has a lot of difficulty quitting, even though both of them have been smoking for ten years, and both of them smoke twenty cigarettes a day? The answer lies in what I have already discussed above, and they are our **THINKINGS.**

The only thing you will have to change in your life is your current perception of who you are, what others think of you, and finally who you really are?

While you can change your thoughts, your environment and your business strategies, what you will have to realize is that you will not be able to change your own Law of Nature - it is perfect. Therefore, we must respect this and begin to adhere to its dynamics of governance, without violating it. How can nature affect our success?

This is a valid question, but after a deep analysis you will understand that we as human beings are constantly breaking the rules, laws and eternal processes of life on a daily basis.

Without straying too far from the subject, observe carefully and observe how the beautiful rhythm of nature is doing its duty daily without any discordance and interruption. In the same way, we have much to learn from nature. Deviation from the truth leads to dismay and failure, and breaking the Laws of Nature will bring despair - in short, macrocosms and microcosms are indifferent.

The decisions you make in your life will determine the outcome of your future events. Always think first of what you are about to do or intend to do, and in taking this action, how it will affect you.

Don't act on impulse, but rather keep calm, remain silent and try to keep a deep silence as long as you can. It is simply amazing what can be achieved through silence and introspection.

I suggest that you undertake a form of relaxation exercise, such as meditation or even yoga, to help you achieve peace and success.

Good judgment is a perfect indicator of wisdom through the expression of the power of the intellect through the faculty of discrimination.

If you have clearly recognized your madness, then you must admit mistakes and bad habits. If it bothers others or affects their health, their conscience, their financial status, their family, their well-being and their peace of mind, then you should ask yourself, ``How much better would I be without it? If you don't benefit from this, why do you even take it or think about it?

Understanding failure

Reason is the greatest enemy faith has.

This is a fact because it is very likely that both the believer and the unbeliever will resort to this statement in support of their respective arguments.

You have already been familiar with the dualistic nature of life, and as such human reason will find both "pros" and "cons" for good and bad action respectively.

It is then that you have to learn to be guided by the inner voice of "consciousness". The following emerges from this innate power, intuition, truth, peace, righteousness, love, non-violence (in words, deeds, actions and thoughts) and the power of discrimination. These attributes have their existence in the soul.

This is the greatest truth that you cannot afford not to know. Effort is proportional to grace, but I wish to add that success is proportional to effort only when one has learned to appreciate the qualities of love.

Whatever you do, put in all your effort and do what you do with absolute love.

Those who are willing to take risks succeed. It is a known fact that young people are more adaptable to change. As we age, it becomes a little more difficult and difficult to bring about change and the ability to adapt to a wide range of comfort zones. Before it's too late, eliminate the problem from the beginning - don't let it gnaw away at your system. Like a virus, act and remove it from your system immediately.

The fact is that we are born perfect (I don't mean this in the physical sense of the word), but the rigors of time `adulterate' this perfection, and therefore the infinite possibilities that lie lurking within us become blurred.

However, what makes us superior is that there is but one great and lovely gift which is ours all the time, and this is our extraordinary power to discover, develop and declare that we, as human beings, have the capacity to reach great heights, if not greater, already within us is the infinite source of energy which is clearly ours!

"We are helpless victims of our own desires and needs."

The ultimate goal

Most people, as I am sure they will agree to do everything half-heartedly and the reasons for that have been covered.

They do not use their full potential, mainly because they have not understood the power of the mind.

We are often attracted or forced to do things that bring us pain. Temporary pleasures bring sadness, and consequently most of us, through fear or even lack of trust, are 'forced' to throw in the white towel.

This need not be the case, because this book gives you the ability to overcome these obstacles by delivering words so powerful that you can change your circumstances. It's about time you looked at your mind's graphs very carefully.

After introspection, now is the time to remove the dirt and, through the use of the power of discrimination, distinguish what gives you lasting happiness rather than sadness.

The bottom line is that you have to exercise control over your thoughts.

The following is included to guide you on your journey to wealth, health and happiness.

- Avoid stopping at all the bad things you have done.

- Repeating wrong actions over and over again becomes habits. Just be careful not to repeat those actions again.

- Don't think of yourself as a failure. Use failures as a means to success - don't give up until you reach the desired goal.

- You will have to erase the furrows from the bad habits you have created by creating good habits. If you are lazy, decide to be positively active and assertive - set yourself tasks or goals and make sure you reach them.

The fact that we resist change shows that we have our own "comfort zones" and this is the result of our thoughts. Why do we resist change? The simple answer to this question is fear of change.

Change means that we have to let go of what `feels' is `right' for us.

The question that remains to be asked is: what is best for you? This is a difficult question, and the answer is that until we are completely satisfied with ourselves, then even a millionaire who wants an extra million is a beggar. How many of us are happy?

We look for instant results, and when we don't "see" the results, we become discouraged and give up. It is my belief that when you desire something for the right reasons then nothing will stop you from acquiring it - this is the eternal law.

Paving Your Way to Success

I wrote this book with only one intention in mind and it is to help you understand and finally help you realize the Power of Mind.

What you will soon discover is a series of steps that you have to follow very strictly to determine your deeply rooted desire. These steps are not monumental tasks, but simple guidelines to begin with.

1. Believe in yourself and in the power of affirmations. Successful people become successful through the constant use of their willpower. Do not be afraid of setbacks in the early stages. Transform failures into success through wisdom, strength, and faith.

2. Believe in the philosophy of 'simple living and high thinking'.

3. Hold nothing against anyone. Strive to overcome your past grievances and move on. Try to forgive everyone 'pain never helps'.

4. Honesty is the golden rule. Observe the silence, meditate and remove all negative tendencies from your system (i.e. jealousy, ego, hatred, fear, etc.). Stick to the following principles: love, truth, righteousness, peace, and nonviolence (don't even hurt anyone with your words, actions, and thoughts).

With absolute determination, it is important that in order to be successful you associate with people who have already achieved it.

To appreciate the purpose of this book, it is vitally important to examine the following points. It will make more sense to you know why success or failure depends on how you define yourself:

IMAGE: The better you feel about your self-image, the greater your chances of success. Image does not necessarily mean appearance; it also has a deeper meaning and connotes reflection.

The image you may have of yourself is more likely to come from what you 'think' of yourself. The internal environment that I have discussed above can play a crucial role in determining your ultimate goal.

EMOTIONS: It is obvious that our thoughts and feelings, which are subtle, have a great influence on our lives. The best way to counteract these subtle forces is to exercise silence during meditation and relaxation exercises.

It is advisable to do a form of exercise to keep the mind positively active. Of course, the second benefit is health. A healthy body serves as a perfect `vehicle' to do it well.

Every individual seeks happiness in life. Now the same happiness we seek becomes a joy once found. This joy can overcome 'bliss' by simply joining in.

LOVE. You must share love in what you do and you must love what you accomplish daily in your life. In the silence of the night, introspect and learn to improve your life (in words, deeds, thoughts and actions) and thank the supreme universal energy.

Along with what has been said above, good communication skills, interaction and good relationships are the way forward - this is ultimately the essence of the virtues and character that will make you successful.

Develop a harmonious personality, and remember what was mentioned at the beginning, always use loving words - words can bring peace or start a world war.

Conditioning your mind effectively will allow you to reap the rewards. It is very good practice to scan your daily thoughts just before going to bed, and note this in your progress book.

Set goals and objectives daily and work on them until you achieve them.

Time is the most precious good in life, use it wisely - lost time is lost life. When you decide to achieve success in your life, make sure you have no contradictory thoughts. If you learn to consciously control and thus implement the inexhaustible powers within you, you can accomplish much more.

Language is nothing more than the expression of thoughts and experiences.

Communication plays a vital role in your overall success, much less in your daily life. Through the power of knowledge, you can achieve specific goals, because the secret of our strength lies in our knowledge. When you have an idea that is viable, you need to focus on it one hundred percent.

Do not tell it to the world - there is no need for such a "spectacle". Think about it and turn it into a "product" that has a solid foundation. Without a firm foundation, a building has no chance of standing.

The Law of Prosperity

There is no harm in the success of desire and all other good things in life, but assured rest, desire that leads to the persistent feeling of lack or incomplete can be dangerous.

If for some reason desire leads to sleepless nights and frustration - it's time to STOP whatever it is you're doing.

Contentment is the one true factor in affirming your abundance. A selfish desire leads to total failure!

Spiritual law is very powerful.

That said, you should strive to follow the following principles daily in your life. Be always good to everything around you, don't be treacherous and deceitful. Beware of the ego and be true and sincere.

Consideration is incredibly important, so always remember the unlucky people, and extend your helping hand as much as you can to those who deserve it.

Training your mind to achieve great heights is not a difficult task. In your free time, do not waste your energy; instead, spend time contemplating the power of your innate self.

Meditate daily and visualize your success

and goals. My friends, the power of the mind is simply amazing, the fact is that we don't even use the power of the mind.

10 percent of it in our daily lives - now, based on this scientific understanding, imagine what you could accomplish if you used the remaining 90 percent?

Just as you savor food when you chew and taste it, do each and every act with a sense of gratitude and do it voluntarily and, most importantly, with joy.

Do NOT blindly follow every little impulse, learn to reflect and to distinguish between what is temporary and fleeting and what is lasting, what is essential and what is not, between what is pleasant and what is not.

Self-conquest will give us what we seek. It must be stressed that balance is also an essential ingredient in their quest for success and wealth. You must allocate time for yourself and your family or that of your loved one. Permanent happiness must be independent of a changing environment.

Don't become a workaholic or a "rich businessman" in your pursuit of success, let alone your attempts to succeed sincerely in life.

Do not stray from the path of justice or the Law of Nature. It is so much fun to witness success and wealth, and the joy that sprouts is beyond doubt. However, if happiness, joy and success all come at once at the expense of your health, then I fear it is a terrible waste.

The way to be rich is by employing the following virtues, which is our true nature, and is found not only in human beings, but in everything around you: Truth, justice, peace, love, and nonviolence. Ask yourself, if all human beings apply these attributes consistently - the world and its inhabitants would prosper.

We must approach all our work (including problems) or duties with concentrated energy and thus execute it with absolute perfection. Strive to do all things (small or however small a duty or job) in an extraordinary way. Do all your work and duty with LOVE and enthusiasm, and observe the results. Never try anything half-heartedly; you will not progress in life.

The power of words

The power of words can have a very strong impact on our minds and our lives.

Before I continue, I would like you to reflect on the following question: Could someone remain silent at all times?

Don't let anyone know what's inside your heart and mind for the simple reason of not being verbally or emotionally expressive? However, I can say with certainty that each and every one of us is a silent talker. We talk to ourselves in many ways and situations, sometimes we hurt ourselves and other times, talking in silence brings a wonderful smile to our faces!

Therefore, communication is very important in life. Words are powerful and, depending on how they are pronounced, can influence our daily thinking processes, actions, behaviors and our view of life as a whole.

Of course, depending on how they are used, the effect words can have is quite incredible, they can be used to persuade, inform, hurt, relieve pain or even start a war! Words spoken with great emotions have the power to bring about changes that can accelerate the healing process of the body!

This enormous power lies in the meaning of the words, what they mean for the person listening to them. Much more than simple communication, truth, falsehood and the infinite nuances between them, words have the power to manipulate other people's thinking and behavior.

It is our interpretation of words that is the true cause of our emotional reactions.

Words pronounced softly, selflessly, innocently and with absolute love are those which are indelibly lodged in our being from where they produce their overwhelming agitating effect on the soul. Therefore, it is very important to use words selectively and appropriately at any time and in any situation.

Modern science is beginning to appreciate the powerful effect words can have on our bodies when used in the form of prayers or even affirmations. Did you know that through conscious effort, we can create a very strong willpower in ourselves?

Affirmation for success:

I will pursue it relentlessly, for it is my birthright to succeed. I am powerful and will get what I need when I need it. I am destined to reap the fruits of my actions and I will share my joy of success with everything I know.

Benefits of Affirmations

- Self-esteem and a positive attitude
- Helps you achieve goals and objectives

- Improve your memory and skills
- Helps build inner self-esteem (willpower, confidence and character)
- Can help you evolve spiritually

Words spoken with softness and love will be attractive and provoke instant admiration. Wealth is in itself a word, and by itself means nothing.

The only factor that gives wealth to the word, the meaning, is the intellect. The wealth of information is nowhere to be found, but it is within us at all times. Intellect is cultivated through logic, and the main point is that dry logic and philosophy can often be counterproductive. Therefore, it is essential to communicate effectively, because in the search for wealth, you will need to sell your business or your company through communication (words).

However, communication alone will not correspond to your success.

The power of unconditional love

It seems to me that people have forgotten the true value, meaning and definition of the word love.

You can exclaim and say what love has to do with wealth! It is naturally difficult to define true love, let me explain, let me say you want to learn to swim, you read books about the art of becoming a good swimmer, but until you jump into the pool under the guidance, the true meaning of swimming has no real value or meaning.

You have to taste the fruit to know its true

flavor, as the saying goes.

Selfish love rooted in desires that are by no means harmonious is the most damaging, and if you dive into acquiring your goals through deception, slander and against all noble and ethical principles, it is best to keep this book.

Those who understand love live in harmony and it is natural for these individuals to attract what they have wanted to achieve.

The greatest power of attraction in every sense of the word, be it a relationship, a business, or a friendship, is love.

As a budding entrepreneur, remember that

the attractive power of love is incredible: you must practice compassion and watch your business grow and prosper.

In achieving any form of success in life, it is pertinent that no matter what happens, don't force your success on anyone - avoid selfishness, pride and don't impose your power on anyone - it's a mistake to do so.

It is crucial that by enriching yourself, you do not abuse your newly acquired "power". When power is used properly, know that you have achieved glory.

Final Feelings

This book is written with the intention of allowing you to discern the innate latent powers that lie dormant within each of us.

Opportunity seekers cannot really give themselves the luxury of "choosing and choosing," but must learn to capitalize on each small opportunity offered to them.

As a seeker, take advantage of opportunities that have the potential to become an indispensable gateway to success: it's about taking calculated, controlled, measured and informed risks.

Rich individuals have created their own careers because they are true believers in success.

These are individuals who cannot stop until they succeed. They are disciplined warriors who wield their weapons of truth, honesty, sincerity, compassion, determination, power, principles, righteousness, wisdom, faith, self-confidence, creativity, strength and skill to reach the heights par excellence.

Life functions strictly according to the incorrigible laws of nature. The reason for this is to establish efficiency, and within the scope of law, the rational intellect in man can be developed for greater efficiency.

They are already rich, however, because of a

lack of understanding of their powerful innate qualities, these attributes that lie in abundance have not found the dynamism to express themselves and manifest themselves.

Finally, do not take life too seriously. Life is a journey made possible for all of us, and if we are willing to give ourselves the opportunity to grow, then life can be a wonderful experience. It is very entertaining, especially when one follows its principles of government religiously.

Be happy at all times, when difficulties arise, laugh at them, and use the dynamic willpower within you to combat them. As mentioned elsewhere, the body and especially the mind is really an amazing instrument that we have.

A state of complete tranquility is possible and there is growing evidence to establish the greatness attained by ordinary people throughout history - it is time for you to use the powers of your mind to achieve your desires.

HOW TO ACHIEVE TRUE FINANCIAL FREEDOM

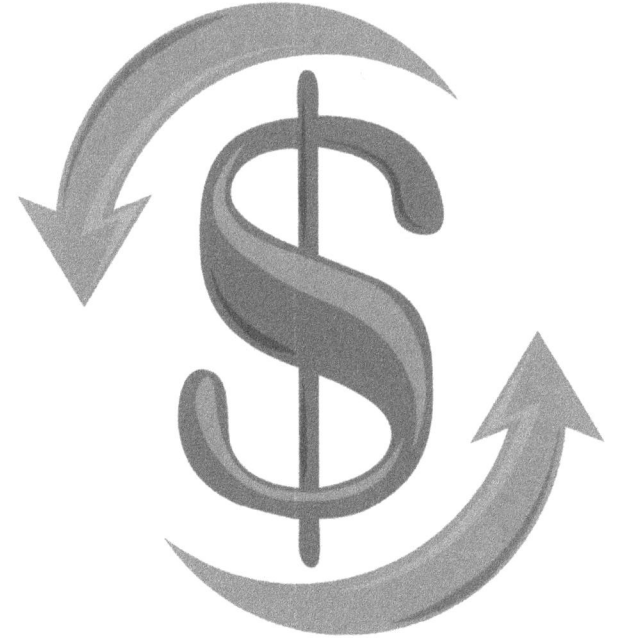

BOOK 2

HOW TO ACHIEVE TRUE FINANCIAL FREEDOM

Chapter 1: What Financial Freedom Means

In the 21st century, the concepts of time and money are being redefined. "Financial Freedom", is a term that has gained a lot of importance in the changing financial scenario.

"Financial Freedom" means the freedom from ongoing financial responsibilities through planned management and asset allocation. It frees a person from a strenuous job by giving them a stable source of income for life.

One should not think that a debt-free person

is also debt-free. However, their prudent asset management ensures that their debts do not become a burden, but only a part of their overhead. In this way, your debts do not stand in the way of your long-term financial goals.

Financial freedom cannot be equated with being rich. It should not be forgotten that excess wealth requires constant supervision. In the long run, a rich man's obligations do not make him "financially free" in the true sense. Thus, financial freedom can be defined as a lifestyle that mixes expenses and income according to individual preference. This makes "financial freedom" more possible and convenient.

Financial freedom is freedom of time

"Time is money," is the general belief in the professional world. This attitude leaves no room for free time. However, financial freedom has changed this concept of work by allowing a person to enjoy leisure without hindering their stable income in any way. The whole concept of "financial freedom" is based on assets and investments that are combined over time to generate money. It takes care of regular expenses and leaves a person with time and money in their hands. A financially independent person is free from the clutches of routine time for money.

Achieving Financial Freedom

To understand "financial freedom" you have

to get away from the traditional concepts of income and expenses.

We have been taught that timely work makes money. Financial freedom" is opposed to this concept of exchanging time for money and letting money work for us. However, despite this advantage many professionals find it difficult to work without a fixed routine.

Therefore, to achieve financial freedom one needs to change their old mentalities and develop a new attitude to making money. One must realize that money is simply the means to an end.

One must also remember that a person cannot be judged by the money he possesses. Unless these misconceptions are cleared up, the purpose of financial freedom will be defeated since satisfaction is the key word for financial freedom.

Similarly, one must also get rid of the negative attitude toward earning money. While excessive demand for wealth makes a healthy relationship with finances difficult, a healthy perception of money is necessary to maintain an excessive balance. Remember that one earns money to achieve ends and therefore it is healthy and normal to earn money as long as one feels an ethical need to do so.

In the end, it can be said that financial freedom is the state of mind that works towards development through a process of self-liberation.

Chapter 2: Realities of Financial Independence

Independence is a state of being that every living being strives to attain, and maintain forever. From the moment a child sets foot in school, he is made to understand that the knowledge he acquires from this point on is for him to make use of his intelligence, to shape his own future.

When one lives with one's parents, one tends to take many things for granted. Once you start earning a living, you are faced with two diabolical aspects: financial independence and responsibility.

Making money is not enough. Many factors arise when one (sometimes arrogantly) decides to separate from the family and move into one's own home. It's true that now you don't have to think twice about buying that extra pair of shoes; after all, there's no parent waiting at home to look at the package in your hand.

But one has to think about the electricity bill that is due next week, the telephone bill that now seems to be on an astronomical level, and other expenses that have to be paid. Money that has been earned after working hours seems to be forgotten. In Economics, we learn that a country grows only through investment. And investment is the direct result of savings.

Similarly, in the case of an individual, his or

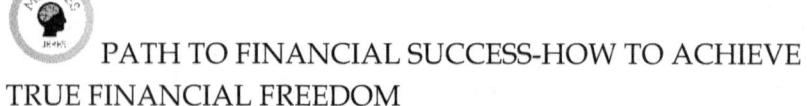

her financial status grows through savings. Some of this savings can be invested in stocks and bonds. And since emergencies and accidents don't come with trailers before them, security regarding health and other insurance must be made.

Women in India have been financially dependent on men for a long time: first as their father's daughter, second as their husband's wife, and then as the mother of their children.

While this has saved them the worry of earning a living, it has also had its drawbacks. A wife abused by her husband is unable to leave him and support herself. Even after the divorce, she is at the mercy of her husband for the support of her children.

But with the changing times, the modern Indian woman knows how to make a living. The power of money no longer manipulates her life.

Living off others brings with it self-contempt and ridicule. Therefore, everyone should work towards financial independence.

Chapter 3: Begin Your Journey to Financial Freedom

To achieve financial stability and security in life, you have to plan and work hard over time. But to make things a little easier for you, here are the most important and time-tested features that could help you reach your financial goals.

Health is Wealth (take care of yourself)

This may seem immaterial, but it is very relevant. Good health ensures that not only do you have the physical and psychological vigor to meet and overcome the challenges of your life, but it also ensures that you will be there to savor the success of your dreams come true.

So get regular check-ups with your doctor, exercise regularly and maintain a healthy diet. And start early. The less careful you are now, the harder it will be to make up for it later.

Define your vision

Defining your vision of your work and life is crucial to your success. What do you want? Is it financial independence, to be your own boss, more security for your family, a solid launching pad for your children? Whatever it is, you must always be your vision in focus.

Reinforce the vision and your role in many ways, and in times of trouble look to it for guidance and comfort.

Invest your money wisely

Although your basic income should come from your current job, don't limit yourself to this. You should try to increase your income by investing your money wisely and profitably.

You could finance or start a business that you are passionate about; otherwise, you could invest in safe market options.

Save Your Money

A good way to build a solid financial foundation is to adopt the old savings mentality. Set aside a certain percentage of your income for savings on a regular basis, and set aside this money every month, every time you receive funds or get paid.

A convenient way to avoid compulsive buying and the trap of poor budget management is to always remember to pay your savings account first. This avoids unnecessary expenses and covers any contingencies that may arise. Although the interest on a savings account is lower than some other investments, setting aside savings is the safest option.

Power Trait-Spend your money wisely

Differentiate within your expenses and avoid
strangers. Before any purchase, ask yourself
if you really need it. Be true to yourself and
your vision: "Do I really need that?" Only you
can answer this question, but you must be
true to yourself and your vision of financial
independence.

Chapter 4: Tips to Ensure a Successful Financial Independence Plan

Even if you have determined a set of financial plans for yourself, whether it's market investing, real estate or retirement, you should try to coordinate these plans to maximize your earnings.

To help you achieve this, here are the 7 crucial steps for financial planning that will allow you to reach your goals, within the time frame you require, with tax benefits and minimal risk:

1) Emergency cash reserves: Always set aside 3-6 months of your salary in an account from which you can withdraw money in the short term without incurring any penalties. For any unexpected short-term expenses, try to avoid using credit cards and use this cash instead.

2) Risk management: Insurance is the safest form of risk management. Therefore, insure your car, your home and other important assets. You may also consider life insurance to help compensate for loss of income and pay off debts in the event of your death. While you are finalizing your insurance option, always choose the type of insurance that fits your needs, and work out the amount of coverage needed that is affordable to you.

3) Estate Planning: The basic features of an estate plan are a will and a durable power of attorney to provide for your medical and financial care. For larger estates, you may also require a living trust, marital trusts and charitable remainder trusts. These ensure that your assets are maintained and passed on to future generations.

4) Goal setting: This is the framework for coordinating your financial plan. Whenever you receive an investment offer, refer it to your overall financial goals. Ask yourself if it is conducive or productive "to", and fits "to", your goals. This commitment to your goals will help you stay focused over the long term.

5) Investments: You need to have a personalized asset investment plan to meet

your objectives and keep the element of risk within the limits you consider acceptable. Without this, your investments will be subject to the vagaries of the economy rather than being driven by your requirements.

6) Retirement plans: Income to supplement your social security will come from defined contribution and benefit plans. During your working life, try to make as many annual contributions to these defined contribution plans as possible. These funds grow rapidly as a result of tax deferral, and since they are obtained directly from your salary, they are relatively painless.

7) Tax planning: This means taking advantage of all the possible tax deductions and tax-deferred plans that the law allows you, as well as using tax credits wherever you are eligible. A good tax plan can save you thousands of dollars in taxes.

If you feel that you cannot handle all of this on your own, seek the services of a paid financial advisor or financial coach to design a comprehensive plan according to your assets and needs.

Remember: Your financial security depends on properly coordinating these separate steps to create wealth.

Chapter 5: Working Toward Financial Independence

Many of us can talk about financial independence but the question is how many of us actually achieve it.

Very few percentages of us know how to make a sound plan and even fewer are able to be disciplined in executing the plan. Be careful and consider a money management program that will help you become financially independent.

Any type of financial planning begins with

proper money management. As you build your plan, be sure to work on two important aspects. First, address the issue of finding the fund that will support your plans and second, get the money planned in such a way that your goals are met.

This money will help you keep the opportunities that are important to you. You might be a little surprised to find that each of us has some sort of money management in place. There are several methods to carry out good money management. It is important that you have an organized approach to the plan and that you get the most out of the money. Focus on identifying your expenses so you know exactly how much to invest.

If you set a goal, it will give you a purpose for investing. Your plans may overlap, so be aware that your goals may overlap.

For example, your retirement plan may overlap with your investment and money management plan.

By now you should have realized that money management is important to future financial goals.

Please stick to a realistic money management plan. Consider how you would achieve the funds. Your goals should be specific. Prioritize your goals to make the path easier.

We are often fooled by a few pre-conceived notions such as living in the moment. We do not realize that there is a future waiting for us. It is important to have an organized approach.

If you don't have an organized approach you may find yourself in some kind of trouble.

You would have to pay extra taxes. You would expose yourself unnecessarily to financial risks.

Lack of funds for your children's higher education. Unsafe aging due to lack of planning

And just the opposite would be the case if an organized money management plan had been made at the right time.

The best result of proper money management is that you are able to meet both long and short-term expenses.

Chapter 6: New trends towards financial management

Economic insecurity is rapidly increasing in the hearts of people who, faced with the possibility of near bankruptcy due to the rising cost of living and the lack of availability of well-paying jobs, are focusing their attention on alternatives, in the marketplace, that will help them to provide for themselves and their families. Therefore, many are looking for any secondary source of income or planning security measures, to support them in case of financial emergency such as the loss of their job.

Others who are already suffering at the hands of social trends are desperately trying to make ends meet and are looking for an opportunity to restart their careers. There are also others who, following the market's guidelines, have managed to accumulate money and are trying to take advantage of their good run, hoping that their future years will be safe.

High Demand Services

That is why it is very important to choose the right type and the right profession. Whether it is a "sit at home" type company or a rigorous field company, nothing else ensures success except its market demand, even in the midst of a large-scale economic crisis.

Since today's world is completely governed by the powers of technology, especially the computer, having a job that keeps you in control of the evils of your job, such as identity theft and general computer problems, is a sure way to find success.

Just as with cars, people use them every day, but they don't know how to maintain and control them. So when things go wrong with computers, no matter how adverse the situation, they will be in high demand.

The best chances of success

So while anyone with a little luck and research can achieve success, people with experience in information services, sales and advertising, or those who are amateurs have a guaranteed chance of success.

The possibilities are even more favorable for small business sole proprietors, since they can use these products on their website to make more money.

Where to look

If you are looking for a healthy victory, then the best option for you is to join hands in partnership with a solid and reputable company, which will help you maximize your profits and help you on your way to a safe and economic future. But before you partner, analyze the company's reimbursement plans and support systems so you can get the best and safest deal from this company.

Chapter 7: Money Matters

With the rapid rise in cost and standard of living, bankruptcy is becoming a fairly common phenomenon - loans, credit card fees, honoraria, etc. - the list goes on. If you don't know how to handle your finances and the stress builds up, you may start to feel that filing for bankruptcy is the only way out.

It is important to understand that this should be your last resort. Before that, you should try counseling and debit card management services and better budget management.

You can also check out debt settlement plans and see if they work for you. Get a counselor to help you find things. But remember that a debt settlement plan will only give you a break. It won't be real and it will make all your problems go away.

You should find a counselor with enough experience. Getting references from people you know is a good idea. The debt counselor will negotiate with your lenders to lower your fees and interest rates.

Second, he or she will also help you consolidate all your debts into one amount. That way, you don't have to worry about managing your payments. You will only have to pay one amount due. He/she will help you get your paperwork and applications in order. All this can help you regain your financial position in a relatively short period of time.

Of course, there are some minimum requirements to get into the program. If you qualify for the program, your monthly budget will be crossed out and a required amount of money will be set aside for your payments. Systematizing things will help you get back on track.

If you're tired of paying the bills that are piling up in front of your face, it's time to rethink your life a little. Enrolling in the above program is a good first step. It will give you a new and positive direction in your life.

It's crucial to managing your loans properly and if you can't do it yourself you shouldn't hesitate to ask for help. It's important to do these things right, if you don't want to jeopardize everything you care about.

Money management is a very important skill. One needs to be taught the importance of saving money and planning a budget from the beginning of life. Be careful with the steps before you have to learn these lessons the hard way.

But if you do get into trouble, don't think twice about hiring the help of a debt counselor. They will give you a plan for your specific, personalized needs. Choose your plan wisely.

One of the most popular plans can get you back on your feet, financially, in as little as five years.

But remember, you have to want to get out of trouble and stay out of it.

You have to have a strong determination to keep your finances in order and not splurge on things you can't afford in the end.

If you do get a second chance at your financial life, don't waste it. Learn to be prudent in money matters before it's too late.

Chapter 8: Distinguishing Between Wants and Needs in Life to Achieve Financial Freedom

Financial freedom and security come from regulating your needs and wants wisely.

Money offers security, but it also takes away your security if it is spent on the wrong things. To deal with this paradox, it is necessary to understand and follow the basic differences between needs and wants in life.

It is important to handle money in such a

way that you do not have to beg and borrow from someone else when there is a shortage of it. These situations can be avoided if you can avoid certain luxuries in life and instead concentrate on saving money to meet life's basic needs.

If you don't have enough money to lead a normal and comfortable life, you will end up leading an inhibited and unpleasant life. You will also end up doing the wrong job and this will make you unhappy and unsatisfied. If there is no security in your life, you will also become less active in your life. It will also prevent you from doing what you really want to do in life, limiting your options and restricting your lifestyle.

The luxuries in life can be largely avoided as long as you have the basic needs in place.

Luxuries are add-ons and can wait for some time as long as we have enough money in our pockets.

This may seem restrictive to many people. They might even argue that it doesn't make sense to wait for a fantastic future when you have money to satisfy all your needs and desires. First of all, you must understand that money cannot guarantee you anything in life.

Money is not an end in itself. It is up to each person to handle money wisely to satisfy his or her ends. You must be strict with your money and spend it only on things you cannot do without.

This logic applies not only to adults, but also to students and children. The value of money must be perceived at a very young age so that your whole world does not revolve around making money. There are other things in life that are not just money.

If you know exactly what you want and what you want to become in life, you can work to get it and get things out of there. Once you are financially secure and independent you can live life the way you want.

This does not mean that you live a luxurious life spending money on unwanted things. By taking into account the difference between desires and goals, you can lead a full and uninhibited life.

Chapter 9: Organizing Your Debt for Financial Freedom

The latest data released by the Federal Reserve, the organization that tracks and records all monetary affairs in the United States, reveals that Americans owe more than two trillion dollars on their credit cards and that the total debt of every person in the country amounts to more than seven thousand dollars.

These staggering figures for credit card debt in the U.S. are bound to affect everyone. So what are the solutions available? You could start by following the suggestions below, which will help you effectively manage your financial responsibilities: Organize your outstanding debt - Start by taking stock of any and all revolving obligations you have. This would include all your credit and debit cards. Tabulate and record your liabilities based on payment schedules, bills, etc. Accounting for applicable interest rates calculates the exact amount you owe.

It is important to know the interest rate on your monthly debts, as this is the ongoing cost you incur against ongoing debt each month. Therefore, it is beneficial to you if you can pay off the loan by charging the highest interest rate as soon as possible.

So while you're making payments, try to send as much as possible to the lender with the highest rate, even if it means you're left with only the minimum payments due on the rest. This way, once the debt with the highest interest has been paid off, you can follow the same policy for the loan with the next highest interest rate.

Negotiate for lower interest rates - try to maintain an immaculate payment history and then call or meet with your lenders and ask them to lower your interest rate. Because it is expensive for lenders to find new customers, if your creditworthiness is proven, they will always try to keep you. Therefore, most lenders will owe customers in good standing to enjoy the reduced rates. However, once they agree to lower your rate, be sure to pay your bills on time; otherwise, they may withdraw the facility and raise the applicable interest rate again.

Use cash when you can - Because it is much easier to use a card than to carry cash or write checks, most of us get into the habit of using cards even if they attract fees. So try to cultivate the habit of writing a check and paying cash rather than instinctively using the credit card.

Always keep in mind that a credit card purchase is not a gift but a loan. So be well advised when using the card: prefer not to use the card at all if you cannot afford the responsibility.

Remember that it is better not to spend on everything than to spend so much that it starts to hurt you.

If you can organize your finances, minimize

your costs and make them proportional to your earnings, you will be sure to put your tour finances in order and avoid any problems in the future. If you put your mind to it, financial freedom is not such hard work, and it is well worth all the effort.

Chapter 10: Six Ways to Teach Children about Money and Financial Markets

If you plan to teach your child to learn how to manage money, then the best way to do so is to start paying off your debts soon. When money matters, kids need to have a first-hand experience. If they do, they will understand what it takes to make the exchange.

If your child wants something from you, instead of buying it, give her the money. You must realize that it is important for your

child to know how to handle money.

When a child reaches a certain age, you should realize his or her inclinations and let the child handle the money on his or her own. Let the child buy his or her own basic needs, such as school supplies. But make sure the child knows his or her limitations. As a caregiver you should keep a sharp eye on his activities.

The next step would be for you as a guardian to establish a budget for your children. Children, no matter how young, have the ability to keep a notebook in which they can write down the money they have and the money they have spent. Make sure your children know their future goals and it's your duty to make sure they achieve them.

As your child grows and matures, open a savings account for them - you'll be surprised how great this can be! It's very satisfying to see compound interest add up. Make an extra effort and show your child by graphing how the account grows. And show him that if he keeps doing it, what the count will be like after a few years.

Have her play a major role while you make a major purchase, such as a dishwasher or a car. Let him know that the amount of research that goes into a new purchase The process of discount comparison and negotiation is important and you will learn this. Make sure your child is with you on the actual day of the purchase.

Your children will be privileged if they have a gift for the business world. Increase the value of the stock and over time if they start owning some stock it could improve. The rise and fall of prices would be interesting for young investors. So we owe them full freedom.

Chapter 11: Financial Independence for seniors

The government-initiated reverse mortgage program has been a blessing to many seniors. The plan, which allows people aged 62 and over to exchange a portion of their home's equity for tax-free money and does not have to be repaid while they are alive, makes it convenient for them to lead full and unyielding lives even when most of the country is plagued by rising expenses in all spheres of life.

Moreover, the effects of such expenses are multiplied when it comes to the older generation, because they have to deal not only with property taxes, but also with general expenses such as health and household.

Thus, this ends up making the lives of the elderly anything but relaxed and peaceful.

Increasingly high land taxes are becoming a burden to these elderly people. It is especially problematic for retired professionals for whom two months of savings equals a small amount of tax due.

This tax problem is becoming the cause of many of them leaving their homes in their 20s and 30s because of inability to pay. This is where Kaye Financial Corporation, one of Michigan's leading mortgage companies, has been of great help to these seniors.

In light of the fact that most of these people are forced to survive on a certain amount of given income, they are forced to compromise on important factors in their lives to meet the rents on the homes.

But now with this new reverse mortgage scheme, they can use the extra money to live a full life, without worrying about how to get resources to survive, even after retirement.

This is especially beneficial because the money is provided according to the person's needs. It can be sent in full in a massive amount, once a month, or in small amounts when needed.

Thus, it becomes advantageous for everyone according to their needs.

Also, since most loans are off-limits to seniors, reverse lending comes as reassuring news to them, since there are no income, health, or age requirements attached to applying for it.

Thus, such schemes provide older people with a sense of well-being, freedom and security.

In addition, they can use the money from this reverse mortgage plan to pay taxes, rent, bills, and other expenses such as the mortgage, so they can live a life without commitments.

So it can be said that the reverse mortgage plan is then the best thing that could have happened to these senior citizens, as they will now be able to continue living their lives to the fullest extent of their wishes.

Chapter 12: Financial Independence and Retirement Planning

Financial independence is essential for all of us after retirement. We all want a comfortable and relaxed life in our old age. Unfortunately, most of us cannot have the kind of life we wanted after leaving work, simply because of lack of money.

In several situations, people have to continue working even after retirement, simply to meet basic needs. The unhappy circumstance could have been different with a certain amount of careful and easy preparation and investment.

These points can allow you to have the financial independence and life you wanted at a later age.

1. The position you aspire to in the end - Remember that the vital section of any aging plan is figuring out the position you want in the latter part of life. Most of us have no idea what life we want in old age, and so we jump into old age schemes without a proper mental goal set in our mind.

2. Wish List - Just as you don't drive a car without having a clue where you want to go, don't plan without thinking. When you take any retirement plan, list all the ones you wish to have after you leave work. List the type of residence you want, the type of car you want, the type of life you want and so on. Don't miss anything. Write down everything down to the last detail.

3. Keep the sheet of paper somewhere more accessible. That way you can see it as much as possible. This process will gradually set the goals you have for retirement and old age on your mental levels. Then, you will gradually form concepts for achieving those goals simply by seeing them and possessing them mentally.

4. Calculate the money needed for the goals - Calculate the amount of funding needed to make the goals a reality. Then look for the assets and investment policies, which can get you there. I will suggest that you get to know all the retirement plans and plans for old age. Then you will be in complete control of the future.

Most of us leave the various aspects of our retirement plans to a money management corporation. But you handle it yourself. Check out the books that deal with investment policies and how to make money.

These points can help you achieve a financially free life in your later years.

Chapter 13: Freedom Has a Price

For anyone who is planning, or going, to start a home-based business, there are some basic conditions and warnings that come in small print, and about which potential recruiters never say much. But it is imperative that you pay due attention to these basic truths.

First, remember that you will always have to make some sacrifices. You will have to spend money, time, and energy to get any business off the ground. Most recruiters misrepresent the opportunity when they insist that anyone can do it, not to mention the high failure rate.

This means you'll have to sacrifice some or most of the time you would otherwise spend doing the things you enjoy or in the company of friends and family. This will undoubtedly lead to stress and resentment and you need to be prepared in advance to handle the consequences.

In addition, you will need the extra energy, beyond your normal quota for your regular job, family and home, to do the things necessary for your business. So you need to tap into your extra reserves: develop your drive to succeed and stay motivated by telling yourself that it will all be worth it in the long run.

As for the financial sacrifices, there are ways to gradually absorb the burden or even eliminate it completely, but in advance, you need to set aside some money to get things going.

The strategy is to be able to see these sacrifices as something positive and productive. So you have to be optimistic and consider them as investments for your future and your independence.

Consider the advantages of prudence and strength: don't be discouraged by initial failures, but learn from them. You can make your sacrifices and failures the foundation of your success.

Your success is what you make and give to yourself. You can think of it as your reward, as something that has already been done in your name, but your part is to deserve it, to make it yours. So go out there and look for your success that is waiting for you to achieve it. There will be times when you will be tested, but you will have to grit your teeth, clench your fists and squeeze. At times like these, just close your mind to all the negative elements, and press to keep your goal and your vision in mind. This is all much easier said than done, but it is also the long, hard road to success.

Chapter 14: Setting Goals for Financial Independence

The first step you should take while managing your money is to have a financial goal. The New Year is an ideal time to help you make some important decisions. It's a time to review your financial goals. Your goals will help you move forward with your finances.

You should have something to work for every day. You should have a planned budget and use these goals you have set as your roadmap. These financial goals help motivate you and encourage you to save.

Without a proper plan it is difficult to get anywhere, so it is important to be well directed.

If you don't have a financial goal, you will never be able to achieve financial independence. You need to put your finger on the things you need to achieve. Make a list of the things you want. Your list can start with the first step of being debt-free; you can continue to owe by starting a retirement account, saving enough to sponsor a home for yourself and other basic needs.

Don't let this entire stop you from writing down everything you want and want to include in your financial planning. In case you're looking for new furniture or a trip to Europe, include that too.

These are money goals that are achievable. Be sure to prioritize your wishes. You must realize that getting out of debt is of the utmost urgency, whereas a tour of Europe can wait.

There are certain goals that we work on constantly, and there are some that wait for certain goals to be met before they can be executed. It is important to set time constraints for the fulfilment of the objectives.

Take for example that there may be about 25 years before you retire, so you would want to be debt-free in about 6 years. Work wisely on your goals. Remember that you are always open to changing them.

Your next step would be to break down your goals into short-term goals. When we break a big task into small steps, it helps us accomplish them better. It makes the task easier. Let's see how this would work to get us out of debt. We need to do one task at a time.

Success and prosperity!